Original title:
A House of My Own

Copyright © 2025 Creative Arts Management OÜ
All rights reserved.

Author: Natalia Harrington
ISBN HARDBACK: 978-1-80587-032-6
ISBN PAPERBACK: 978-1-80587-502-4

Glimpses of Grace

In a nook where socks unite,
Dust bunnies dance in daylight.
Cups of coffee spill their dreams,
While the toaster silently screams.

Pillows whisper tales untold,
Of adventures brave and bold.
A cat that thinks it's queen of all,
Takes her throne on the bathroom stall.

Echoes in the Eaves

Mice write letters, tucked away,
In the walls where shadows play.
The fridge hums a secret tune,
While the clock laughs at the moon.

Chairs that creak with every wink,
Join the dishes in the sink.
The broom sings songs of dust and cheer,
While the dog just snores nearby, my dear.

The Tapestry of Togetherness

Worn-out shoes left by the door,
Mismatched socks in every drawer.
A quirky rug that greets the feet,
With patterns that can't be beat.

Walls have laughed and shed some tears,
Shared whispers with our friends and fears.
Each corner holds a memory bright,
Of silly dances in the night.

Embraced by Earth and Sky

A garden grows of weeds and cheer,
With gnomes that giggle, never leer.
Frogs croak out their nightly song,
While fireflies dance and play along.

The sun spills lemonade on the ground,
Where clumsy ants are always found.
A hammock sways, embracing dreams,
While life bursts forth in vibrant beams.

Cradle of Creativity

In the corner, a pile of paint,
A canvas stretched, perhaps a saint.
Splashes of color dance around,
While my cat claims the throne, unbound.

With crayons stashed in every nook,
I'll draft a tale that's off the hook.
The fridge, my muse, with drawings stuck,
Keeps my quirky thoughts in luck.

The Hideaway of Heart's Desires

In a closet, secrets swirl and twirl,
A treasure trove of dreams unfurl.
Socks are magically mismatched now,
A fashion statement, take a bow!

With snacks piled high like mountains tall,
I hide from chores within these walls.
Each nibble feels like sweet success,
As I escape my daily stress.

Stronghold of Serenity

In my fortress of pillows, I take a seat,
With a blanket cape, I feel quite neat.
Netflix streams my royal decree,
While the world outside just can't see.

Tea spills, as I laugh out loud,
The chaos outside can't make me cowed.
I'm queen of my realm, not a care to lend,
In this quirky kingdom, I won't pretend.

The Keep of Quietude

In the room where silence reigns supreme,
I plot my schemes, like some wild dream.
The washing machine hums a tune,
As I scribble rhymes by the light of the moon.

Beneath a blanket fort, I can escape,
Like a pirate ship, I shape my cape.
Though piles of laundry beckon my name,
In this hideaway, it's just a game.

Chamber of Cherished Memories

I found a sock; it's bright pink,
Crayon drawings on the kitchen sink.
Grandpa tried to play the flute,
Now there's music in my boot.

The cat once thought it was a chair,
Sat on the couch without a care.
Spilled some juice, oh what a mess,
Laughter echoed, I must confess.

The Hearth of Hopeful Horizons

A pot of soup, too hot to eat,
Dancing noodles, a tasty treat.
The bread I made, it looked like goo,
But I served it up with lots of stew.

The wallpaper peels, just like my dreams,
Patterns shifting in silly schemes.
A light bulb flickers, it's lost its fight,
But it still shines in the middle of the night.

Pillars of Belonging

My old chair creaks, it's full of tales,
Of secret whispers and playful gales.
Under the stairs, a treasure chest,
Filled with odd shoes and an old nest.

The goldfish stares with a knowing glance,
While the dog continues his daily dance.
Walls that giggle when you touch
Hold all my dreams, and still, it's too much.

Parlor of Possibilities

The sofa's gone but left its fluff,
A kingdom made of cushions, tough.
The old clock ticks, though it's a fake,
Always late, it's a jolly mistake.

Kites hang low from the mantle piece,
Tangled up like a giant fleece.
In every corner, echoes of cheer,
Make the world feel warm and near.

The Rhythm of the Roof

Above my head, the shingles dance,
While squirrels plot their little prance.
The rain sometimes plays a silly tune,
While I juggle socks at noon.

The walls creak like they've had too much,
As I hide from the dreaded touch.
Potted plants with noses stuck,
Gossiping like it's all just luck.

The kitchen sings with pots that clang,
While I trip over the cat who sang.
Fridge magnets form a wobbly tower,
As I ponder my next snack hour.

My cozy nook, a laughter spot,
Where laundry shrieks, "Oh, give it a thought!"
Dancing brooms that swish and sway,
In the rhythm of my quirky day.

Sage and Stone Stories

In a nook where shadows play,
Sage and stone come out to sway.
They crack jokes with a little twist,
While I wonder how I missed.

The floorboards squeak with things to say,
Whispering secrets of the day.
"Watch your step!" the hallway cries,
As I try not to trip on pies.

The windows wink with dusty eyes,
While curtains dance, oh what a surprise!
I spot a gnome who's lost his hat,
And my cat starts a chat with that.

Tales of socks and burnt bread rise,
In this realm of playful lies.
Each corner holds a chuckle's worth,
In my cherished space of gentle mirth.

Pillars of Possibility

In a place where socks all disappear,
Juggling laundry, oh what a cheer!
The fridge is a treasure, snacks piled high,
A nap in the corner while the cat walks by.

Walls that listen to my silly dreams,
Echoing laughter, or so it seems.
A roof that dances when the wind blows loud,
My quirks are wrapped in a whimsical shroud.

Every creak tells a story, old yet new,
This quirky realm, not for the few.
The floors might slope, but hearts stand tall,
In my castle of chaos, I welcome all.

Each corner holds a ghost that grins,
My wild adventures, where silliness begins.
With every moment, a spark, a chance,
Here's to the laughter, let's all dance!

Tide of Tranquility

Surfing the couch with popcorn in hand,
Remote control battles, it's quite unplanned.
The garden's a jungle, weeds playing king,
While I plot and scheme for the snacks I'll bring.

Bubbles in the bathtub, they rise and pop,
Rubber duckies laughing, they never stop.
The cat on the windowsill, judging my tan,
As I sip lemonade, dreaming of a plan.

The rug is a runway, with my shoes askew,
Dancing down hallways that feel brand new.
With quirky hats that I find in a pile,
Every step in this space brings out a smile.

In this sanctuary where oddities thrive,
Microplaygrounds keep my spirit alive.
Each moment is goofy, each day a delight,
In the tide of tranquility, everything feels right.

Hearthsong of Belonging

The kitchen's a lab where recipes flop,
A dash of this, then a bubble and pop.
Spaghetti on walls, what a colorful sight,
Dinner's a dance, and it's quite a fight.

The living room's turned into a dance floor,
Music so loud that the neighbors want more.
Bouncing off walls, I twirl and spin,
Even the goldfish joins in with a fin.

Every nook holds secrets of laughter's embrace,
Collecting the giggles that brighten this space.
The fireplace crackles with stories untold,
While cookies in ovens turn a bit too bold.

Together we gather as odd little souls,
Playing board games, embracing our roles.
In this magical realm of whacky delight,
We find our home in the chaos of night.

The Breath of Space

Under the stairs, a secret door awaits,
Leading to treasure, or maybe just plates.
Goblins of clutter dance on top of the shelves,
While imagination is shouting, "Explore yourselves!"

The yard's an adventure with bugs and some weeds,
Building a fort from unlikely needs.
Blankets and branches create a tall tower,
Where dreams are invented in spring's finest hour.

The sun makes an entrance through curtains askew,
A symphony spins, mixing old with the new.
Every cranny and crevice holds moments to share,
Life's funny little quirks float around in the air.

So take off your shoes and run wild in this space,
With laughter as currency, we decorate grace.
In this breath of joy where the silly resides,
We all find our haven, where love never hides.

Solitary Symphony

In my nook, I host a dance,
A sock and broom, they take a chance.
The cat leaps high, it stole the show,
While I just sit and watch the flow.

Echoes of laughter fill the air,
As I debate with my own chair.
The fridge hums tunes of bygone snacks,
While dust bunnies launch their sneak attacks.

A sandwich sings a salty tune,
As I pirouette with a big balloon.
Here in my realm, all's quite absurd,
Who knew solitude liked to be heard?

With walls that giggle, I take a spin,
In this grand hall where I always win.
I'll share a joke with my old lamp,
And laugh all night with this raucous stamp.

Where Memories Reside

In a corner, the old chair creaks,
It whispers tales, it softly speaks.
A stack of books with tales untold,
Wear my memories, bright and bold.

My fridge is a vault, holding surprises,
Yesterday's pizza has some disguises.
I stroll through halls of mismatched shoes,
Each step a moment, each heel a muse.

The windows shout with their daily glare,
Curtains chuckle at the gossip we share.
Pots and pans rattle with culinary dreams,
While I concoct my most dubious themes.

In this cozy chaos, joy does abide,
Where every quirk is perfect, side to side.
Collecting laughter like stamps in a book,
Each recipe different, each memory a hook.

Enclosed by Emotions

Witty walls can hold a jest,
Whispering secrets, they never rest.
A wobbly table joins the fun,
While I, the chef, just can't outrun.

The microwave hums nostalgic tunes,
As I dream of vegan raccoon buffoons.
Chairs conspire to have a seat,
And lose their balance, oh what a feat!

My couch plays host to epic debates,
About chocolate cakes and their weighty fates.
Lively laughter seeps through the cracks,
Even the broom feels it under itsax.

The whole place bubbles with quirky flair,
As I serenade the dust in the air.
With joyous antics all around,
In this zany space, I feel profoundly sound.

The Soul's Safe Haven

In a quirky room where dreams can stray,
An old cat wanders, leading the way.
My slippers dance, with mischief in tow,
As I navigate this delightful show.

Frames hang crooked, with smiles so bright,
Each portrait laughing at my new hair plight.
The sun blinks in, like a loving friend,
In this laughter-filled space, no need to pretend.

My desk holds treasures, like half-eaten snacks,
And scribbled notes of comedic hacks.
A mirror guffaws at my latest hairstyle,
Reflecting joy in its golden smile.

Within these walls, my spirit roams free,
Crafting laughter like a wild jubilee.
This whimsical place is a delight unconfined,
Where each little quirk is perfectly aligned.

Dwelling of Dreams

In corners hide my socks and shoes,
A wild parade of daily blues.
The fridge is full of random snacks,
And ghosts of old take playful jabs.

The cat's my roomie, curiously bold,
To steal my chair, she's always told.
With every nap, she takes a leap,
To claim my bed and watch me sleep.

The walls may creak, the floors may sigh,
Yet here I laugh, and never cry.
In this quirky maze, I spin and dance,
Each laugh a twist, each chance a chance.

A coffee cup that spills with glee,
Reflects the chaos that's part of me.
This space, a stage for every jest,
My comical castle, I am blessed.

Sanctuary for Solitude

My throne's a chair with rips and tears,
Where I plot my dreams and daft affairs.
Refusing calls, I strike a pose,
Like royalty in mismatched clothes.

The fridge hums tunes of mystery,
It's a glitchy friend, it sings to me.
In every box, a little chaos,
A buffet of the lost and awkward gloss.

There's wisdom in my cluttered bliss,
An echo of what I dare to miss.
With laughter ringing off the walls,
My kingdom of quirk forever calls.

I wear my blanket like a cloak,
And share my thoughts with every joke.
In this delightfully messy space,
I find my peace, my happy place.

Nest of Whispered Wishes

The cushions argue, who's the best,
My pillow's shaped for every jest.
A fort of dreams, I build it high,
Where paper planes are meant to fly.

With pizza boxes strewn about,
I contemplate this life, no doubt.
The laughter echoes through the halls,
As mischief dances on the walls.

My gadgets beep like little friends,
In this cocoon, the madness bends.
With a dance-off in the kitchen light,
I crown the oven, my party knight.

Each corner's filled with silly memes,
My heart resides in colorful schemes.
A space for wishes, hopes, and quirks,
A happy mess where my joy works.

Haven of Heartbeats

In my haven, socks do play,
Their pairs are lost, they've gone astray.
Beneath the couch, I find a shoe,
I toast to all my oddball crew.

The mirror mocks my morning face,
A style that jests at every trace.
With toothpaste spills and coffee stains,
I reign supreme in these domains.

Dance parties break out in my room,
With dust bunnies inventing new zoom.
The ceiling fans spin tales of fluff,
In this sanctuary, there's never enough.

A treasure chest filled with old toys,
Each holds whispers of childhood joys.
In every giggle, a heartbeat's tune,
My heart thrives here, beneath the moon.

Lattice of Longing

In a room stacked high with cheese,
The mice hold meetings shared with breeze.
Posters of past victories they boast,
Who knew they'd be brunching hosts?

The cat is banned from the fun,
Can't reach the rafters, skill's been undone.
They plot with crumbs and plan with flair,
A banquet fit for all furry dare!

Every nook, a secret treat,
With saucers of milk, a blissful feat.
The decor's a mix of cheese and time,
Laughter rings loud, like a nursery rhyme.

At the window, a dog does peek,
His face a picture of comic cheek.
He dreams of a life where he, in disguise,
Might join the bash, much to his surprise!

Beneath the Attic Sky

Dust motes tango, swirling up high,
In a world where socks dream to fly.
Old toys gossip, whispering tales,
While the broomsticks plot grand scale gales.

The chest in the corner wears a grin,
Filled with treasures where fun begins.
Brave boots on journeys to lands so grand,
While action figures make their last stand.

A sunbeam strikes just right, oh dear,
Lighting the mischief brewed in here.
Forgotten cookies from who knows when,
Hold the secrets of this crazy den.

As the clock ticks an offbeat tune,
Furniture dances beneath the moon.
It's a party of shadows, laughter, and might,
While the house hums soft, in the dim twilight!

The Secret Pockets of Place

In a closet where old coats reside,
A snail holds court with eyes open wide.
Jacket pockets filled with notes from friends,
Each scrap a story that never ends.

A shoe hums softly, shuffling along,
Tapping the rhythm of a snappy song.
While unpaired socks have a debate,
On the merits of mismatched fate.

In the back where the dust bunnies roam,
Forgotten hats form a cozy home.
Top hats dangle, speaking of airs,
While caps share secrets, none have declared.

Beneath the creak of a quirk-filled floor,
Imagination opens a hidden door.
Where chairs hold a council of wits and glee,
And laughter rings bright like a key!

Mosaic of Moments

Paint splatters tell stories on walls,
The laughter of paintbrushes fills the halls.
Colors clash in a vivid embrace,
Doodles of dreams dance all over the place.

The fridge has a gallery of art,
With magnets boasting a culinary heart.
A pizza slice, a running man,
Each piece a masterpiece, an odd little plan.

Curtains sway to the chaotic beat,
While pets sleep, doing their best to compete.
In this wild patchwork of love and cheer,
Every misstep's a headline we hold dear.

As dusk turns to evening, mischief begins,
Friends gather 'round for whimsical spins.
In a world of wonder, we giggle and play,
Creating tales that forever will stay!

Edifice of Elusive Dreams

I built a castle made of cheese,
With walls of crackers, oh what a tease!
My moat is filled with fizzy drinks,
A fortress where only my cat winks.

The drawbridge drops for pizza night,
Toppings galore, what a glorious sight!
I invite my pals, they all arrive,
To munch and laugh, we feel so alive.

My towers made of candy, what a sight!
Gummy worms dangle, oh, such delight.
But watch your step on those jelly stairs,
One wrong move, and you're lost in layers!

At sunset, we dance like silly fools,
On giant marshmallows, oh, how it drools!
In my whimsical world, we spin and sway,
Creating dreams that never decay.

The Cottage of Kindred Spirits

In a cottage made of pancakes stacked,
We sip on syrup, joyfully snacked.
The roof's a fluffy cloud of cream,
In this land, we live the sweetest dream.

Friendship blooms in the garden bright,
Where chocolate flowers sway in delight.
Every giggle's a sprinkle of fun,
Under the golden, syrupy sun.

The walls are stories, each one a joke,
We gather 'round, no need to provoke.
With laughter bubbling like soda pop,
In this cottage, we never stop.

We roast marshmallows on a candy fire,
Sharing secrets that never tire.
As the moon winks down on our glee,
In our sweet haven, just you and me.

Refuge of Reverie

In a gingerbread haven where dreams reside,
With licorice curtains, oh, what a ride!
Each nook is filled with giggles and glee,
A realm of silly fun, just wait and see.

The ceiling's spun sugar, a treat to behold,
With popcorn chandeliers, oh, so bold!
We sing to the moon, our voices all blend,
In this whimsy lounge; the fun never ends.

Our floors are made of caramel tart,
Where each stomp and skip is a work of art.
We tumble and play, no worries in sight,
In this refuge, everything feels so right.

At dawn, we wake to pancake skies,
Where laughter dances, and joy never dies.
So let's wander in this land so bright,
Forever reveling in pure delight.

The Fortress of Fondness

In my fortress, the walls are made of fun,
With jellybean guards, oh, how they run!
We bounce on trampolines, high as the sky,
In this fortress of fondness, we soar and fly.

Each room is filled with laughter and cheer,
With bubblegum carpets, come grab a sphere!
We play hide and seek with muffins galore,
Finding treasures, oh, who could want more?

The lunchroom's a carnival, treats on parade,
With cotton candy clouds that never will fade.
Every moment's a hoot, a wild carousel,
In this place where we let our joys dwell.

As the stars twinkle, we tell ghostly tales,
Of silly adventures and magical gales.
In my fortress, the heart finds its song,
With friends by my side, where we all belong.

Oasis of Open Roads

In my car, I feel like a star,
Zooming past cows and old rusty cars.
Gas station snacks are gourmet delight,
Chocolate bars make the long trip light.

Wind through the windows, music so loud,
Singing off-key, I feel so proud.
Traffic jams turn to dance parties so grand,
Who knew the highway could be such a band?

Rest stops named after odd things,
Like 'Peanut Butter' and 'Lion's Rings.'
I stop for a stretch, pretend I'm a tree,
Who needs a yoga mat? Just let it be!

With maps that confuse and apps that distrust,
Every wrong turn is simply a must.
So here's to the roads that twist and shout,
Adventure awaits, there's never a doubt!

Retreat of Resilience

My couch is my kingdom, in sweats I reside,
In this throne of comfort, I take great pride.
With snacks piled high and shows on repeat,
Why leave the fortress? This is pure treat!

The fridge holds treasures, cold and divine,
Midnight feasts? Oh yes, that's a sign!
Pajamas parade like it's fashion week,
Style is subjective, but cocoa's my peak.

Dust bunnies dance, they're my cleaning crew,
They swirl around like they know what to do.
With popcorn storms and laughter galore,
My humble retreat is never a bore!

Zoom calls in pjs, I ace the disguise,
Pretend I'm in meetings while really in pies.
Here in my realm, where resilience is found,
I conquer the day, in sweatpants I've crowned!

Nook of Endless Journeys

In my corner chair, I travel the seas,
With a book in my hand, I sail at my ease.
Magic carpets and dragons take flight,
No packing required, just read through the night.

Pillows like clouds, I float and I swoon,
With tea in my cup, I look at the moon.
The world outside fades to a whispering hum,
In this nook of mine, I go on and come.

Friends in the pages, they share every tale,
Each chapter brings laughter, sadness, and ale.
From castles to jungles, the adventures unfold,
With every new story, my heart feels bold!

So here's to the journeys inside my small space,
Where I leap through the words at a glorious pace.
My nook is my treasure, my safe happy zone,
In every new story, I find my way home!

The Vault of Vulnerability

In the depths of my mind, I hide every whim,
Where giggles and secrets dance in a hymn.
I keep all my quirks in a sparkle-filled chest,
A treasure of blunders, I know I am blessed.

Under the surface, it's silly but true,
I misspoke last week, oh what could I do?
There's a stash of old socks that don't even pair,
But they hold my hearts, with love and a flare.

Every awkward story, a gem in the light,
Each misstep's a laugh, it feels just so right.
With friends who embrace my peculiar side,
We laugh through the mess, in hilarity, we glide.

So here's to the vault where I stash all the fun,
With hideaways full of joy – oh what a run!
In the chaos of living where joy does reside,
I treasure my quirks and take them in stride!

Shelter Beneath the Stars

When I build my place up high,
I'll slap a roof beneath the sky.
With laundry dancing on the line,
And squirrels serving cheese and wine.

Chairs that wobble, tables quake,
Where every meal's an epic mistake.
A garage filled with dust and dreams,
And cats who plot their own schemes.

With an ice cream maker gone awry,
Creating flavors that make you cry.
Sure, I'll live in total mess,
Yet laugh my way through every stress.

So here's to floors that creak and moan,
And a backyard where gnomes have grown.
A haven where giggles are the best,
In a world that's joyfully a jest.

Refuge of Forgotten Stories

In a nook filled with dust and cheer,
I hide away my old, lost gear.
A sofa born of cushions sprawled,
Where every tale gets gladly scrawled.

Books with secrets yell, 'Oh, read!'
Tangled tales take up the lead.
And pictures scribbled on the wall,
Of my best friends—a canine ball.

Potato chips beneath the seat,
Hide treasures that old socks can beat.
A place that smells of cookies past,
Each flavor a memory that holds fast.

In this space of whimsy and glee,
Where shadows play, and drinks are free.
I'll laugh with strangers, and we'll dance,
In corners where dreams take their chance.

The Abode of Aspirations

In my spot where swagger meets the sun,
I'll gather dreams and just have fun.
With furniture that mismatched plays,
Creating chaos in funny ways.

The pots all whistle, the pans will clank,
As I create my chef's prank.
With flour storms and doughy fights,
Cooking disasters become delights.

A garden with weeds more than flowers,
Taking up space while I lose hours.
A birdbath that's merely a bowl,
Which is, of course, perfect to console.

Where every mishap cracks a smile,
And laughter flows in every aisle.
I'll keep on living, pushing the bound,
In my realm where joy can be found.

Cornerstone of Contentment

In my cozy little den of cheer,
Every corner whispers fun, my dear.
Cushions piled like mountains high,
Where projects fail and laughter's nigh.

A fridge that beeps a jolly tune,
Dancing treats that come out of June.
The ceiling draped in fairy lights,
As I fumble through my nights.

Comfy slippers, two sizes too big,
I waddle around doing a jig.
And never mind the dust bunnies here,
They're my pets, my little seer!

It's my sanctuary, a whimsical crowd,
Where odd is normal, and I feel proud.
In this lair with laughter's decree,
I found my place, my silly spree.

Windows to Wanderlust

Through panes of glass, I dream and scheme,
Each view a ticket, a wild, mad theme.
The neighbor's cat, my travel guide,
Whiskers twitch, on adventures we ride.

A cloud chases an errant sock,
On laundry lines, they twist and mock.
Here I sit, pen in hand,
Sketching journeys, oh so grand.

The world outside, a circus bright,
As squirrels plan their daring flight.
I'll send postcards from my chair,
With tales of snacks and comfy wear.

Windows frame my wild, wild thoughts,
As sunlight in soft splatters spots.
I'm off to Paris, or maybe Rome,
But first—who's that? Oh! It's the gnome!

Corners of Comfort

In every nook, a secret lies,
A stash of snacks, a pile of pie.
I fit right in, like socks on feet,
In my cozy haven, the ultimate treat.

The armchair whispers, 'Stay awhile,'
As I stretch out and flash a smile.
A shifty cat tries to claim my space,
But I've got the snacks, I'll win this race.

Blankets swoop like a superhero's cape,
In corners where I escape all shape.
A rubber duck guards my bubble bath,
As I plot the couch's hilarious math.

With mugs of cocoa and comfy socks,
I observe the world through gossip blocks.
The corners giggle, as I declare,
My quirks, my snacks—beyond compare!

The Architecture of Aspirations

With dreams like blueprints, bold and bright,
I sketch out plans in soft twilight.
A fortress made of cereal boxes,
Defending me from life's hard knocks.

Each wall a canvas, painted with flair,
Expressions flourished, hung in the air.
A moat of pillows, my cozy zone,
Battling boredom—invention is grown.

The ceiling beams whisper tales of cheer,
Of dance parties held when no one's near.
With every giggle echoing high,
I construct my dreams, reaching for the sky.

So here's to the plans, ridiculous and sweet,
To building a world where whimsy meets.
With laughter and grace, my mansion unfurls,
In the joyful chaos, my spirit twirls.

Hearth of Healing

The hearth is warm with tales of old,
Where laughter blooms and stories unfold.
With marshmallows toasting on tippy toes,
We share our quirks, like silly prose.

A couch of fluff holds whispers tight,
As we giggle through the starry night.
The popcorn pops, a jolly surprise,
As the cat performs for our starry eyes.

Tea brews dreams, as giggles rise,
A bubbling pot filled with wisdom and pies.
Huddled together, we dance and sing,
In our cozy corner, we're all Queen and King.

The hearth glows bright, with warmth inscribed,
In laughter's charm, our hearts reside.
Through ups and downs, it holds our grace,
An endless hug, our cherished space.

Journeys Traced by Walls

Beneath the roof where shadows play,
I chase my thoughts that fly away.
Each corner holds a hidden scene,
Of socks and snacks and spaces clean.

The echo of a distant tune,
A dancing broom, a swaying moon.
My puppy guards the front door tight,
Announcing guests with snorts of fright.

A poster hangs, a crooked smile,
It knows that life's a goofy trial.
In this abode, we make our claim,
Each wall adorned with laughter's name.

Food spills and laughter fills the air,
Here's the place without a care.
Beyond the threshold, adventures wait,
Inside these walls, we celebrate.

The Embrace of Resilience

In rooms where whispers weave their tales,
I build my dreams on rusty nails.
The ceiling bends with every hope,
While dust bunnies perform their slope.

A chair with springs that squeak and groan,
It knows my secrets, all alone.
With laughter plastered on the walls,
I dance through life in silly halls.

When storms outside begin to shout,
Inside, we're cozy, there's no doubt.
A fort of pillows, blankets stacked,
We smile through chaos, never cracked.

So here we sit, a merry crew,
With tales of mischief, strange but true.
Resilience found in quirky ways,
This home's a circus that always stays.

The Ageless Shelter

With cracks in the plaster, stories lie,
An ageless shelter under the sky.
The fridge hums tunes, a silly song,
While I trip over the cat, oh so wrong.

Sunbeams dance on the kitchen floor,
As I sneak snacks, just won't ignore.
The floorboards creak, a voice so old,
It tells of laughter, young and bold.

The wallpaper peels with style and flair,
A patchwork quilt beyond compare.
Each window frames a world bang-bang,
Where silly thoughts and giggles hang.

Oh, this place, it never grows stale,
With pets and pals, we spin our tale.
A timeless realm of whims and dreams,
As life flows on in goofy streams.

Reflections in Glass and Grain

There's a mirror that laughs at me,
A face of mischief, not quite free.
With messy hair and mismatched socks,
I ponder life with all its knocks.

A table stands, adorned with crumbs,
As family chatter softly hums.
Each scratch tells of feasts and fights,
Of midnight snacks and silly nights.

The windows show a world so vast,
Filled with memories forever cast.
In every grain of wood, a tale,
Of storms weathered and ships that sail.

So here I sit, in comfy cheer,
With each reflection, more than mere.
For in these frames, our lives entwine,
In laughter's echo, we brightly shine.

Where the Heart Dwells

In a nook where socks collide,
And dust bunnies seem to hide,
I search for snacks throughout the day,
In this wacky hideaway.

The fridge sings songs of yesterday,
While my cat dreams in a sunbeam's ray,
The couch has crumbs like a treasure map,
And right here's my cozy trap!

The wall clocks tick with a funky tune,
Echoing laughter like a cartoon,
With every room a giggling friend,
In this place where joy won't end.

So pass the quirks, let's toast the fun,
In this zany spot, we'll always run,
Where silly moments bloom and swell,
Here's where the heart and humor dwell.

Horizons of Homecoming

Upon the mat where shoes are tossed,
Memories linger, never lost,
It's a circus act when we arrive,
With laughter that helps us survive.

Kitchen chaos as pots collide,
A dance of spices, side by side,
The oven beeps a merry tune,
While we thrash like a wild raccoon.

The couch is comfy, but holds a prize,
Lost remotes and popcorn skies,
With every cushion, a story's spun,
In this place, we're always young.

So here we are, with silly tales,
Trading socks for dreamy gales,
In this patchwork gold that we call home,
Even the walls are free to roam.

Rooms of Resilience

In a room where chaos reigns supreme,
And the vacuum's more like a roaring dream,
I dance with brooms, a swirling friend,
While laundry piles like a mountain's end.

The bathroom mirror shows my best side,
As my hair defies the morning tide,
With every twist, a new surprise,
Frizzier than the brightest skies.

My closet's bursting—a style parade,
A mix of fashion, a grand charade,
It's a canvas of flair and blunders bright,
In this space, there's no wrong or right.

With laughter echoing off the walls,
And playful bounces when duty calls,
In every room, life makes amends,
Where even messes are our best friends.

Beyond the Threshold

At the door where the socks mismatch,
The welcome mat's a jumbled catch,
With each step, there's a chuckle phase,
As we greet life in quirky ways.

Past the gate where the garden grows,
We dodge the weeds and tickle toes,
Every bloom a giggle in bloom,
As butterflies turn the air to perfume.

Under roof beams that sway and creak,
We plot our fun with a wacky cheek,
In shadows where old jokes call out,
And every echo is a joyful shout.

So here I stand, with arms stretched wide,
In this realm where wonders abide,
Beyond the threshold, life's a stage,
Where every day writes a brand-new page.

Light Against the Shadows

In empty rooms where dust bunnies roam,
I've claimed my turf, this is my home.
A cat on the couch, he's king of it all,
While I chase my snacks, I'm having a ball.

With mismatched curtains and floors that squeak,
I dance like no one's here, unique and chic.
An old fridge hums a tune from the past,
Each door I open, brings laughter at last.

The walls hold secrets of whispers quite bold,
Like my tea that spills, turning stories to gold.
I trip on my shoes, they laugh and they cheer,
In this vibrant chaos, I find my frontier.

The Palette of Peace

In shades of chaos, I paint my day,
With splashes of socks strewn every way.
A rainbow of snacks in each cupboard hides,
Cereal for dinner? My appetite guides!

My walls are adorned with frames askew,
A gallery of quirks, my own curvy view.
Each brushstroke of laughter is vivid and bright,
In this funny abode, I twirl in delight.

The couch wears my imprint, it sighs each time,
As I jump on the cushions to make a new rhyme.
A palette of chaos, a stroke of pure bliss,
With every silly moment, I feel life's sweet kiss.

Sanctuary of the Heart

This sanctuary hums with giggles and cheer,
As I search for the remote that keeps disappearing.
With ice cream in hand, I conquer each night,
In my fortress of fun, everything feels right.

The cushions are fortresses, I'm ruler supreme,
With a throne made of pillows, I'm living the dream.
My socks throw a party, they dance on the floor,
While the clock ticks away, I'm never a bore.

This refuge of chaos, where laughter is loud,
Becomes a stage for mischief, I'm royalty proud.
Every chuckle's a brick in my castle's fine art,
This wacky abode, my sanctuary of heart.

The Flavor of Familiarity

In each little corner, a taste of the past,
The coffee's still brewing, it's cheers that we cast.
Spilled juice on the table, a colorful mess,
Each taste brings a chuckle, life's silly success.

Beneath the old fridge, the dance of my feet,
With cereal crunching, it's midday retreat.
My dog is my partner in this frothy delight,
He snatches my snacks, and we laugh through the night.

Through sweet and through sour, we savor the fun,
The laughter like frosting, it's never outdone.
In the flavor of chaos, together we cheer,
In this zany buffet, forever sincere.

Echoes of a Silent Refuge

In a room filled with socks that don't match,
My cat holds court like a royal dispatch.
The walls listen close, they giggle and sigh,
At the antics of life as days flutter by.

The fridge hums a tune, it's quite out of tune,
Bouncing leftovers dance under the moon.
A chair has a creak that's a song all its own,
With a drink in one hand, I call it my throne.

Dust bunnies waltz in the corners unseen,
While I twirl with my broom, like a queen on a screen.
Each morning I stumble, it's quite a routine,
In this odd little castle, I reign like a queen.

Oh, the echoes that bounce off the ceiling so wide,
They share all the secrets the coffee can hide.
I laugh with each creak, every bump in the night,
In this quirky domain, everything feels right.

The Heartbeat of Abode

Beneath the sofa, the remote's gone astray,
I search with a vigor that just starts my day.
The rug starts to chatter, it's seen better days,
While my plants roll their eyes at my indoor malaise.

The clock on the wall ticks with such endless flair,
I swear it's a spy, just a bit too aware.
The cushions conspire in plush, fluffy plots,
As I sink into comfort, forgetting my thoughts.

The bathroom sings softly, the tap gives a sigh,
While the shower curtain waves like a friend passing by.
Each corner has stories that beg to be told,
As I dive into chaos, it's fun to be bold.

In the kitchen, pots gossip like old pals on deck,
While the fridge plays DJ, my favorite disc wreck.
With a dance and a laugh, I whizz 'round the space,
In this playful retreat, life's a whimsical race.

Dreamscapes of Dwelling

In the land of mismatched plates, I take my stand,
With a cup that's unsteady, it's part of the band.
The chairs have their quirks, they wiggle and moan,
But in each little squeak, I find joy of my own.

The bathroom's a jungle, with loofahs that gleam,
Toothpaste performs stunts, it's more than a dream.
The mirror reflects laughter, and maybe a frown,
While I practice my poses, hero or clown.

My bed is a ship in the night's gentle swell,
With pillows like clouds, where I wish I could dwell.
The quilt whispers tales of adventures afar,
As I sail into slumber, my nighttime bazaar.

The walls wear the art of scribbles and spouts,
A gallery of love, where no doubt's allowed.
Here's where the magic meets laughter and cheer,
In the arc of each moment, I'm happy to steer.

Sanctuary of Shadows

In the corners, where dust bunnies plot their delight,
The shadows dance softly, they twirl in the light.
The ceiling has secrets, it giggles and peeks,
As I trip on the carpet and tumble in streaks.

The window's a portal to world's soft embrace,
Where squirrels perform stunts, it's an acrobatic race.
The fridge is a guardian of whimsy and taste,
Baking bits of laughter, no crumb goes to waste.

When I open the pantry, it whispers, 'Surprise!'
With cans full of mysteries that widen my eyes.
The rugs feel like islands in oceans of cheer,
As I circle the room, the laughter draws near.

Underneath the dishes, small treasures I find,
With memories and snacks, the perfect rewind.
In this joyous enclave, where shadows take flight,
I gather my giggles, embracing the night.

Portraits of Shelter

In a tiny box, I keep my cat,
He thinks he's king, and I'm just a brat.
A throne of pillows, his mighty crest,
While I sit on the floor for this crazy test.

The ceiling whispers, 'Watch your head!',
As I dodge the lamp that wants me dead.
Every nook and cranny seems to conspire,
To make my midnight snack a full-on fire.

The paint peels off like a tired old joke,
While I fight the dust bunnies, a mischievous cloak.
Each corner holds a laugh or a tear,
As I trip over shoes in my own little sphere.

So here's to the chaos and all that's absurd,
For I love this wild place, no need for the birds.
With laughter and quirks, it feels like a hug,
In my quirky abode, I'm never a bug.

Tales from the Threshold

The door squeaks open with a ghostly sound,
I tiptoe in, hoping not to be found.
The fridge groans softly, as if to say,
'Why not raid me now, and throw your diet away?'

My neighbor's cat thinks he owns the path,
He sits on my welcome mat, full of wrath.
I step around with a dance and a twirl,
To dodge the furry boss's unfriendly swirl.

Old postcards line the wall like tales,
Of trips I never took, just off the rails.
They smile at me with their faded grace,
While I sip my tea in this crowded space.

Each creak and crack tells a story so bright,
Of all the mishaps that fill the night.
A place made of laughter, where silliness rings,
In this wacky world, oh, the joy it brings!

Lights in the Window

The streetlight flickers like it's lost its way,
While my lamp just hums a soft jazz ballet.
With mismatched curtains, a fluffle of style,
My home is a gallery of quirky guile.

My neighbor claims I'm a bit too loud,
But I can't help it, I'm a vibrant crowd.
Dance parties with snacks, under starlit shade,
While the walls, they chuckle, our fun parade.

Pasta and giggles make for great nights,
As I chase after dreams and take flight on kites.
Every window shines with a sparkle so bright,
As I chase away shadows with every delight.

So raise a toast to the glow, oh so warm,
In this crazy haven where I weather the storm.
With smiles and mischief that never dock,
I'm the queen of my castle, with plenty of stock!

A Dwelling of Delight

Walls of whimsy hold secrets untold,
Where socks disappear, in a fashion so bold.
Coffee spills laughter, a melody sweet,
As I dance with my broom, and shuffle my feet.

Wobbling shelves, and a plant in distress,
Call me the queen of chaotic finesse.
I laugh at the clutter, it's part of the game,
In this quirky retreat, nothing feels lame.

Chasing the dust bunnies, what a great feat,
My vacuum's a monster, my nemesis neat.
I tiptoe around with a wily old grin,
In this playful abode, there's always a win.

So here's to the bliss in my silly domain,
Where sunshine and shadows play joyously plain.
With laughter and nonsense that brightens the night,
I've crafted a haven, where everything's right.

Pathways to Peace

My floors creak like a symphony,
With socks as my secret, a dance for free.
The cat hires a bouncer, he won't let me through,
As I tiptoe around just to look for my shoe.

The walls tell stories of laughter and fun,
While I search for the remote, oh where has it run?
Each corner a treasure, could this be a clue?
Or just the lost chips from last Sunday's view?

The fridge is a wonder, it sings when I peek,
While leftovers stare me down, feeling quite sleek.
I barter with tacos to keep the peace here,
In my abode of antics, there's nothing to fear.

So here I stand, in my fortress of light,
With polka-dot curtains and squares that ignite.
Pathways of giggles unwind with my soul,
In this whimsy-filled maze, I am truly whole.

Angles of Affection

My roof is a hat, quite tilted and worn,
With windows that wink as the sunlight is born.
The corners are cuddly, each angle a hug,
Where dust bunnies gather and happily snug.

The kitchen's a circus with pots on parade,
As I cook up a storm—oh, the plans I made!
The blender's a monster, it splatters and spouts,
Turning peas into smoothies, oh what are those shouts?

My couch holds the secrets of TV galore,
With cushions that eat me, I'm lost in their lore.
I tumble through pillows while trying to see,
The show that the cat's been intent to decree.

So here in my angles, affection's a game,
With laughter and chaos, what's truly to blame?
In this quirky abode, each moment's divine,
With angles so silly, together we shine.

Shelter from the Storm

The roof's a bravado, quite proud and quite bold,
As raindrops tap dance, stories are told.
I gather my pillows, a fort I'd declare,
With blankets for walls, all worries laid bare.

The thunder is raucous, a wild beast it seems,
As I sip on my cocoa, indulging my dreams.
Each crack of lightning, a glow show that cheers,
We giggle in shadows, no room for our fears.

The windows are eye-watches, taking it all,
Guarding my laughter, they stand proud and tall.
I watch raindrops race, each one just a thrill,
While wishing for ducks, a family for skill!

So here in my haven, the wild winds can blow,
With mug in hand, I'm a star of the show.
Forgotten are worries; I'm cozy, you see,
In this blustering storm, it's just you and me.

Dreams Framed by Beams

Sunshine drapes over, a warm golden hue,
My beams are the guideposts, my thoughts they pursue.
Each night I count stars, some shoot like a dart,
While my dreams play games, pulling strings of my heart.

In a world made of laughter, my ceiling's a jest,
Where ideas take flight, oh, they're simply the best!
The floor's a trampoline, as I bounce about,
With socks like a rocket, I soar, twist, and shout.

The walls hum tunes of adventures untold,
While I sketch my next journey in crayons of gold.
My spot by the window is where magic does bloom,
Creating new worlds in my bright little room.

So here's to the beams, the laughter they share,
In this canvas of joy, nothing can compare.
As dreams float and flutter, whimsical gleam,
I dance through my day, on a wish or a beam.

A Retreat of Radiant Reflections

In a nook where slippers dance,
Reading socks take a chance.
The curtains gossip, oh so bright,
While the cat claims the sun's warm light.

A fridge plays tunes, a salsa beat,
With leftovers that talk, can't be beat.
The walls wear stickers from the past,
Memories linger, forever vast.

Chairs swap stories, creaks and laughs,
As dust bunnies do their little half.
A carpet soft as a fluffy sheep,
Where secrets of the pillows sleep.

This place is wild, a cozy zoo,
With mismatched mugs, a quirky crew.
It's not just shelter, it's a spree,
A joyful chaos, come join the glee!

Nurturing the Forgotten Corners

In the corner lurks a sock's lost mate,
The couch says, 'Don't be late!'
An eco-system of dust resides,
With crumbs and giggles as the guides.

A coffee table holds treasures rare,
With coasters stacked like they just don't care.
The fridge is more than food galore,
It's a portal to snacks we all adore.

Behind the curtains, old dreams prance,
While sunbeams throw a wild dance.
A ladder leaning, full of hope,
Suggests a climb, a comical slope.

In forgotten spaces, laughter finds,
The funny quirks that life unwinds.
Each nook a stage for joy to play,
In corners where the silly stay!

Whispers Within These Walls

Within these walls, secrets reside,
Where my left shoe and right shoe hide.
The wallpaper chuckles in a hue,
As the lamp tries to light-up the view.

The refrigerator hums a lullaby,
While the cat rolls by with a sly eye.
The sofa holds a popcorn stash,
With cushions that hold stories in a flash.

Chasing shadows as the sun takes flight,
Whispers in the night, a silly fright.
A clock that ticks in a slow parade,
Convinces me time's all but a charade!

Each crack and cranny tells a tale,
Of misadventures that never fail.
Echoes of laughter, a light-hearted brawl,
In this quirky space, we share it all!

Foundations of Solitude

In solitude, my sandwich sings,
With pickle jokes that joyfully sting.
The chair in the corner plots a scheme,
To host a dance in a mid-afternoon dream.

A stack of books with winks and giggles,
Their spine is bent from all the wiggles.
The TV remote rebels on the floor,
Holding court on who watches more.

The rug whispers tales of wandering feet,
While the coffee pot steams with a heartbeat.
Guess what? The dishes have a plan,
To rise up and form a dish-washing clan!

Each corner blooms with idle chatter,
As time unfolds, and dreams don't scatter.
In madcap moments, here I thrive,
Foundations strong, where fun's alive!

A Dwelling of Untold Tales

In the nook, a chair so bright,
It squeaks and groans, a comical sight.
The cat thinks it's a throne of dreams,
While I just dodge its sneezy beams.

The kitchen's a lab for homemade soup,
With pots that dance and spoons that loop.
I swear the fridge has a mind of its own,
It hums a tune as its items have grown.

The bathroom's a war zone, rubber ducks fly,
As I splash water, oh me, oh my!
The mirror chuckles at my silly hair,
With toothpaste smeared, I'm quite the fair!

Each corner whispers its own joke,
While my vacuum takes a break and yokes.
So here's to the chaos, laughter so loud,
In this quirky place, I wear the crown proud.

The Fortress of Familiarity

My couch is a ship on a sea of snacks,
Where pillows become islands, safe from attacks.
Remote in hand, I conquer the shows,
In my fortress, anything goes!

The closet's a cave where my socks seem to flee,
I swear there's a portal, just wait and see!
Shoes piled high like a mountain of fun,
I make my way through, one by one.

Walls covered with photos, those goofy old days,
Each smile captured, in many bizarre ways.
The ceiling's a canvas for dreams to take flight,
As I laugh and I wonder, oh what a delight!

Here's a kingdom where rules disappear,
Dancing in pajamas, slapping cheer.
So join me here, where silliness reigns,
In my fortress of fun, I'll break all the chains.

Enclave of Eternal Echoes

Inside these walls, echoes of giggles dance,
To a rhythm of friends and their silly prance.
Every corner a story, echoing loud,
In this whimsical space, I'm always so proud.

The garden's a jungle, plants rave and jive,
As my gnome throws parties, oh how they thrive!
With the sun as our DJ, and rain as the tune,
We groove with the daisies; it's quite the boon!

The doorbell's a joker, its chime makes me squeal,
I rush to attend—what an odd little deal!
Who's at the doorstep? A bird? Maybe a frog?
I'll greet them with snacks; let's all have a hog!

In this enclave, where echoes ring clear,
Every laugh adds another layer of cheer.
Join the fun, where the stories unfold,
In a realm of pure joy, we're never too old.

Sanctuary of Self-Discovery

In my little nook, a space to unwind,
Where I chat with my plants, such joy to find.
Each leaf is a buddy, so wise and sincere,
They listen to secrets and cradle my fears.

Beneath the table, my socks disappear,
But my missing shoes? They haunt me, oh dear!
With paper-scrap maps to the land of the lost,
I navigate dust bunnies, whatever the cost.

The walls are my canvas, with doodles galore,
From monsters to puzzles, I create and explore.
A treasure of memories, laughter, and grace,
In this wacky haven, I find my own space.

So let's raise a toast with my juice box in hand,
To the little adventures that life has planned.
This sanctuary, a playground of whimsy and fun,
In the tapestry of living, I'm finally spun.

Luminescence in the Lull

In the corner a lamp, doing the cha-cha,
Light flickers softly, like an awkward ballerina.
The couch is a kingdom, ruled by my snacks,
And the dog is my subject, with legs like planks.

A rug with the pattern of a giraffe in a hat,
Spots sparkle wildly, oh what fun is that!
Mirrors reflect my snacks, brighter than gold,
In this silly palace, I laugh, bold and cold.

The fridge sings tunes, a diet it mocks,
Holding leftovers, and at least five clocks.
The oven's a wizard, baking my dreams,
While the toaster just pops, it seems to have schemes.

In this realm of oddity, where whimsy prevails,
Each little corner tells funny tales.
Through the halls, I dance, laughter my guide,
In this light-hearted paradise, I'll always abide.

A Space for Serenity

In a room full of pillows that giggle and squeak,
I find my own solace, quirky and bleak.
The curtains perform dances, swirling in delight,
While dust bunnies plot their next daring flight.

A chair with a heart, it hugs me so tight,
Telling tales of the day, through the soft moonlight.
Ola the plant gives a sly little wink,
As I ponder my life while sipping cold drink.

The clock on the wall has a mind of its own,
It ticks just to tease, and leaves me alone.
My socks have a party, mismatched they gleam,
In this zany haven, I follow my dream.

Walls lined with laughter, with doodles galore,
Here, nonsense and joy knock upon every door.
I cradle the quirkiness, warm in my nest,
In this space of delight, I do what I jest.

Shadows of Solitude

In the corner sits a shadow with flair,
It talks to the light, like they're quite the pair.
The floor sings a creaky, nostalgic song,
While the dust dances wildly, where it doesn't belong.

My chair wears a cape, it's ready to soar,
With snacks at its side, it's never a bore.
The walls are a canvas, showcasing my glee,
Each doodle a chapter in this book of me.

The vacuum's a monster, I bravely face it,
Waging a war, oh how I embrace it!
But when it retreats, I sigh with a grin,
It knows how to clean, but I'll never let it win.

In shadows I linger, where laughter is keen,
This castle of quirks, adorned in green.
With solitude wrapped in a riddle so bright,
I find joy in the quiet, my heart takes flight.

The Cradle of Memories

In a nook piled high with remnants of cheer,
Old socks tell stories, when no one is near.
A table with crumbs, a feast from the past,
Where thoughts float around, in a swirl so fast.

The chair squeaks its secrets, from late nights gone wrong,

It giggles at whispers, and joins in the song.
From cartoons at dawn, to snacks by the fire,
Each bit of nostalgia fuels my heart's desire.

The closet's a treasure, with shoes from my youth,
Stepping back in, I find all my truth.
A hat with a feather, once worn with great pride,
We reminisce softly, as memories glide.

In this cradle of laughter, where time holds its breath,
Each object a gem, in the dance of my quest.
With folly and fun, I cherish it all,
In this haven of whims, I forever stand tall.

The Haven of Heartbeats

In a quaint little nook, where the cat takes a nap,
With cushions galore, it's the best kind of trap.
The fridge is a shrine to leftovers long gone,
We dance with the dust bunnies, laughing till dawn.

The plants have opinions, they whisper at night,
They judge my bad TV choices, oh what a sight!
Every creaky old floorboard sings its own tune,
As I trip on the carpet, I waltz with the moon.

The neighbors might wonder, what happens inside,
As I host wild parties with no one to hide.
A sock on the door means "please come have some fun,"
With snacks that are questionable, but laughter's a ton.

In this haven of chaos, I'm never alone,
With each quirky moment, I've brightly outgrown.
Here's to the madness, the giggles and glee,
In the heart of my haven, I'm truly just me.

The Lattice of Life

In my patch of the world, where the odd socks parade,
I plant silly fantasies, watch dreams cascade.
The fridge hums a tune of forgotten delights,
As I dance in the kitchen, what a funny sight!

My bookshelf's a jungle, it teases and plays,
With novels unpicked since the good old days.
The mirror reflects all my lost combs and keys,
As I trip on the rug, feeling quite at ease.

A window that creaks tells secrets it knows,
While I juggle my snacks, oh how the laughter flows!
With plants speaking softly, like whispers of fate,
This lattice of life feels like love at first rate.

I cherish each moment, these quirks I adore,
With friends made of shadows, we're never a bore.
In this lattice of laughter, under stars that shine bright,
I find my own rhythm, my delight, my light.

Where Silence Speaks

In the haven of hush where the time stands so still,
Even dust bunnies chatter, oh what a thrill!
With walls bearing witness to giggles untold,
It's a sanctuary built from the brave and the bold.

The clock ticks a joke, in its own little way,
While I squeegee the windows to keep clouds at bay.
Each corner a canvas of quirky delight,
Where silence erupts in the air with pure light.

I've crafted a space where socks don't need pairs,
And floors are just stages for dance without cares.
The couch holds the secrets of evenings so grand,
As whispers of laughter fill this humble land.

In this cozy abode, where silence holds court,
I find all my rhythms, and comfort is short.
So here I'll reside, in this whimsical peak,
Where silence takes charge, and the heart skips a beat.

My Fortress of Dreams

In the fort made of blankets, my kingdom appears,
With snacks in the nooks, and no room for fears.
Each pillow's a guardian that laughs in delight,
As I plot all my schemes in the soft glowing light.

The walls are adorned with my wildest of hopes,
A gallery of giggles and colorful scopes.
The fridge holds my treasures, leftover and bright,
While I crown myself ruler of all that feels right.

With a sippy cup scepter, I reign with a smile,
Where laughter resounds and I rest for a while.
The clock's running amok, yet I don't mind the race,
In this fortress of dreams, I've found my own pace.

When the world outside tumbles, I stay cozy within,
With whimsical musings that dance like the wind.
This fortress of laughter, where joy feels supreme,
Is my very own castle, my whimsical dream.

Cascades of Comfort

In a nook where my slippers dance,
Socks and snacks join in the prance.
Pillows pile high, a soft brigade,
Cushioned laughs in my fabric shade.

Walls that creak with secrets bold,
Whispers of mischief, stories told.
Cards and games scatter the floor,
A fortress built for fun galore.

Hiding from chores that loom and glare,
The vacuum cleaner is in despair.
Chillin' with cookies, just me and my cake,
In this laughter zone, I do what I make.

So here I lounge with comfy zest,
In my whimsical keep, I feel blessed.
All the world can wait and spin,
While I'm the captain, let the fun begin!

Refuge from the Rushing

When life is fast, I slow the clock,
Pull out my snacks, give time a mock.
Books stack high like a cozy wall,
Who needs a throne when I have this hall?

Coffee cups are my trusted mates,
They share my secrets, never hate.
In my whirlwind, I find a chair,
With fuzzy blankets beyond compare.

Robots roam, but I am still,
Turning off noise is my ultimate thrill.
Pajamas reign, the formal wear stays,
In my castle, I rule the play days.

Here in my bubble, I float on air,
With a giggle and grin, a life so rare.
The traffic jams can honk all they want,
I'll keep spinning in my comfy jaunt!

Tucked Away Treasures

In a corner where giggles twirl,
Toys and trinkets around me swirl.
I claim my world, a treasure chest,
With oddities that put me to the test.

Socks with holes, oh what a show,
Magical marbles in a neat row.
Stickers riddle my funky walls,
Where laughter echoes and joy enthralls.

Drawings that inspire, colors collide,
In my realm where no rule can bide.
An umbrella turned fort, oh what a laugh,
As clouds of imagination do their path.

Here I stumble upon quirky finds,
Navigating life that twists and blinds.
In a jungle of nonsense, I parley the fun,
With randomness reigning, I've already won!

Chronicles of the Unseen

Within these walls, a tale unfolds,
Of socks that vanish and secrets untold.
In the blur of days, I sip and munch,
Writing my history with a playful crunch.

Dust bunnies chatter, they laugh with delight,
While sticky fingers take flight at night.
Each surface holds a daring goal,
Transforming chaos into my soul.

Jars of candies, a sight to behold,
Each flavor craves a story retold.
As toys play hide and seek without care,
This place is my vision, my glorious lair.

Throw in a cat with a sly kitty grin,
Dancing like nobody's watching, let's begin.
These chronicles bloom where the laughter's seen,
In my playground of dreams, I'm the real queen!

Traces of Light in the Dark

In a nook where shadows creep,
I found a light that makes me leap.
A sock on the ceiling, a cap on the chair,
Housekeeping's a sport, do I look like I care?

The fridge hums a tune, it spills its own snacks,
I dodge hungry giants, oh, what a few hacks!
A dance on the floor with a broom in my hand,
Who needs a partner when dust bunnies band?

The clock ticks like laughter, gives time a good shove,
Each tick is a secret, I can't help but love.
When night rolls around, the fun starts to spark,
In a world where the silly leaves traces in dark.

The cat looks at me like I'm quite the odd fry,
With my disco ball dreams and disco ball pie.
Life's more a joke when you're spinning around,
In this jester's abode, giggles wear the crown.

A Canvas for Dreams

Brush strokes of laughter paint the wall,
With a dash of confusion, I trip then I fall.
A couch that swallows all secrets we share,
And cushions that giggle like they just don't care.

This space is a riddle wrapped up in a grin,
Where the art of relaxation is where I begin.
A masterpiece formed with each cozy chair,
And abstract ideas float high in the air.

With socks mismatched like a colorful fest,
I tire of the sofa, so I take a quest.
To find the last cookie, oh, what a thrill,
In this quirky abode, I'm king on the hill!

Each corner reveals a whimsical twist,
A spark of surprise, nothing's amiss.
A canvas of chaos, it feels just so right,
In my gallery of giggles, I sleep well each night.

Sanctum of Solace

In my fortress of fun, where socks do reside,
An army of plush toys stands by my side.
I crown myself ruler of pie crumbs and fluff,
In this realm of retreat, I never have enough.

With bubble wrap armor, I'm ready to play,
The walls echo laughter, it's a bright, jazzy day.
The carpet's a beach, where the sand is pure joy,
And the sun beams of sunshine, oh what a ploy!

Here, I can mingle with imaginary mates,
Discussing grand plans while debating on plates.
The tea, it is magic, a potion divine,
And by the way, is there cake on the line?

In the peace of this space, with giggles we blend,
Sanctum of solace, where quirks never end.
It's home to the funny, the wild, and the free,
A treasure trove of nonsense, come dance here with me!

Hearthstone of Hopes

Gather 'round at the kookie fire pit,
Where marshmallows dance and the laughter's a hit.
With slippers that squeak, we roast silly dreams,
A heartwarming laugh's better than all the ice creams.

The walls stick with tales of adventures we've spun,
Where jokes are the currency, and puns weigh a ton.
In a corner, old pillows loom like big pals,
Whispering secrets from silly night owls.

The wallpaper flips to reveal a surprise,
A mural of monsters with glittering eyes.
They guard all our hopes with a playful, bright flair,
In my cozy abode, there's always sweet air.

So come take a seat, we'll brew dreams anew,
In this hearthstone of hopes, there's always a view.
Where laughter's the warm hug that never runs cold,
And friendship's a story that's ever retold.

www.ingramcontent.com/pod-product-compliance
Lightning Source LLC
Chambersburg PA
CBHW070307120526
44590CB00017B/2588